A New Catechism of Socialism by Ernest Belfort Bax
Prism Key Press | www.prismkeypress.com

ISBN: 978-1463650513

A New Catechism of Socialism
Socialism
Ernest Belfort Bax

Preface

The object of the following short treatise on the Principles of Social-Democracy is to afford students and expositors of the subject a comprehensive view, such as we are bold to say has not hitherto appeared in this or any other language, at least in anything approaching the same compass, if at all. The little "Socialist Catechism," by our deceased comrade and friend, James Leigh Joynes, is now nearly twenty years old; and was, from the first, never intended as anything more than an elementary guide to the "man in the street" on the more salient points of Socialist economics. It therefore bears no sort of relation to the present work, which, though necessarily much less elementary, aims at giving a complete view of modern Socialist theory and practice in all their bearings. While the economic basis is dealt with at sufficient length, and, we hope, with the necessary clearness and thoroughness, we have not confined ourselves to this alone, but have endeavoured to show the bearing of Socialist principles throughout all the main departments of human thought and action. Our sketch in this respect has necessarily been slight, but we venture to think that the suggestions embodied in the following pages will be sufficient to enable any intelligent reader to follow them up for himself. We have not attempted to deal fully and completely with any one of the points treated of, but we have aimed at giving, as briefly and concisely as possible, the chief arguments in support of the Socialist view, and at pointing the general trend of the Socialist movement. Experience has frequently shown us the need for such a work, and it is in the hope that it will accomplish the useful end we have set ourselves to serve that we commend it to the active propagandists of the Social-Democratic Party.

A New Catechism of Socialism.

What do you understand by SOCIALISM?

> By Socialism we understand the system of society the material basis of which is social production for social use; that is, the production of all the means of social existence — including all the necessaries and comforts of life — carried on by the organised community for its own use collectively and individually.

But is not society at the present time organised, and does it not now carry on the production of these things for its own use and advantage?

> By no means. Production is carried on to-day purely in the interest and for the profit of the class which owns the instruments of production — by which we mean the land, the mines, the factories, the railways, canals, ships, docks, machinery, and, in short, everything the main object of which is production in the economic sense, i.e., the creation of things for human use.

Is it not just, then, that the means of production should be used in the interest of the class which owns them?

> Certainly, so long as class ownership exists — which is the same as saying so long as classes exist. Therefore Socialism would substitute social ownership of these things for class ownership, and this would also involve the abolition of classes altogether.

You speak of classes, but surely it is individuals who own the instruments of production?

> It is true that individuals are the owners, but these individuals form a class bound together by common interests, as against the rest of society.

Now does the ownership of the instruments of production constitute a class? Are not members of all classes in a greater or less degree owners of these things, as, for instance, the workman who owns a spade, or has a few pounds in the bank, as well as the middle-class millowner or the aristocratic landlord?

The word class is used in many ways. For instance, we speak of the professional class, the clerical class, the military class, the leisured class, the artisan class, the labouring class, &c., as well its of the upper and the lower classes. But this does not alter the fact that society is separated into two main divisions or classes, one section which, for all practical purposes, possesses all the material means of production, and another section which has no effective ownership in, or control over, these things. The possession by a workman of a few small tools, such as a spade, a sewing machine, or a typewriter, for his own personal use does not take him out of the working class, as, in the present stage of industrial development, such things are so infinitesimal in comparison with the great means of production enumerated above as to be of practically no account. The other senses in which the word class is used refer only to subdivisions of one or other of these two great classes.

But are these the only senses in which the word class cans be use?

There is another more technical sense in which the word is used, but this also will be seen on examination to merely designate the historical phases of the two main classes referred to. The great distinction between classes in the past and those in the present day, is that in the past, men were born into a certain status of society, involving subjection or dominance as the case might be, whereas now class is for the most part a question of the possession or acquirement of wealth. The class-ship into which a man is born is sometimes called his "status"; the class-

7

ship conferred by wealth, which is necessarily much more fluctuating than the former, has no technical name.

But, admitting that society is, as you say, divided into two great fundamental class divisions, do not these two sections imperceptibly shade off into each other, and are they not inextricably mixed?

Superficially, yes; but on examination it will be found not to be so. The question as to which of these two divisions a man belongs to may easily be determined by whether he possesses or does not possess effective control over the labour of others through the possession, or if not the actual possession, the control of the means of production. We do not deny that at the point of contact between these two classes it may not be always easy to draw a sharp line, any more than it is easy for a naturalist at the point of contact to draw a line between the animal and the vegetable kingdoms; although no one doubts the validity of the distinction in general.

Then do you propose that all these means of production which are now owned by individuals, by this class, as you say, should be made the property of the Government, like the Post Office and the telegraph system are in this country, and the railways as well in some others, or that they should be owned by municipal bodies, as water-works, tramways, gas-works, and so on, are in many cases already?

No, Socialism does not mean mere Governmental ownership or management. The State of to-day, nationally or locally, is only the agent of the possessing class; the Post Office and the other State-owned businesses are run for profit just as outer businesses are; and the Government, as the agent of the possessing class, has, in the interests of its employers, to treat the employees just as other employees are treated. The organised democratic society contemplated by Socialists is a very different thing from the class State of to-day. When society is organised for the control of its own business, and has acquired the possession of its own means of production, its officers will not be the agents of a class, and production will be carried on for the use of all and not for the profit of a few.

But how does the possessing class, as you term it, derive a profit from business enterprises which are State-owned?

In many ways. In the case of concerns administered by the National Government, the profit generally takes the form of relief of taxation. In the case of businesses conducted by municipal bodies, on the other hand, the propertied classes make their profits by way of interest on loans advanced to the municipality for the purchase of these businesses, and in being relieved of the rates which, otherwise, they would have to pay.

But if Socialism does not mean Governmental, or State, ownership of the means of production, and if, as you say, such ownership is generally in favour of the class whose ownership of these means you object to now; what do you mean by Socialism?

We mean the establishment of a political power — in place of the present class State — which shall have for its conscious and definite aim the common ownership and control of the whole of the world's industry, exchange, &c. The entire means of production thus being common property, there would no longer be a propertied class to make a profit out of interest on loans or in any other way, and the property qualification which now divides society into two classes being thus swept away, classes themselves would disappear.

But as a beginning might not the nationalisation or municipalisation of some industries be made use of for the common benefit?

9

Yes, this can be done, but only to a limited extent, and even to that extent it is very difficult; because the propertied classes being in power take care that as far as possible all national or municipal businesses shall be managed in their interests.

Do you, then, oppose the nationalisation or municipalisation of any industries under existing circumstances?

By no means. In any case even under the present class State, the national or municipal ownership of any business helps, as do also the trusts, to prepare the way for the complete socialisation of all industries.

Then, are we to understand that this common ownership and control of all industries is all that is meant by Socialism? In a word, is Socialism merely an economic theory?

No. Socialism is an economic theory because the economic conditions form the material basis of human society; but Socialism is much more than that, it embraces all the relations of human life. The establishment of Socialism means a complete change in society in all its aspects. The economic conditions directly determine the political conditions; less directly, but none the less certainly, the ethical conditions; still less directly, the aesthetic — although, since art expresses itself in material things, and works through material processes, it here also must exercise a powerful and even a dominating influence. In the region of purely intellectual theory and speculation the influence of the: economic conditions is not directly felt at all, but often considerably so indirectly, seeing that these conditions are the source of many distorting influences, which under present circumstances powerfully affect men, and prevent there seeing the truth in logical, philosophical, and scientific matters. In short, although we do not deny that human intelligence can influence or modify its environment, yet such influence or modification has hitherto usually coincided in the long run with an equal (and often a far greater) influence of the environment upon itself. Action and reaction are inevitable, and are never separated in this connection, although one side or the other may be the predominant factor. We will, therefore, now proceed to elaborate in greater detail the points raised here.

The Socialist View of Economics.

In the first place then what has Socialism to say with reference to purely economic relations?

> Economics divides itself into pure or abstract economics and economics as developed in the concrete in the course of historical evolution. Abstract economics takes no account of the modifying influences of the human mind, whereas in dealing with economics historically full consideration is given to these.

In which category do you place the economic relations of to-day?

> While these necessarily have their place in the historical development, they also lend themselves to be treated in the abstract, and we will now proceed to so consider them.

Will you, then, define some of the terms we so often find in treatises on political economy? For example, how do you define WEALTH?

> Wealth comprises all material things which serve to satisfy human wants and desires. Economically wealth may be defined as such of these things as are practically limited in quantity or are the result of human labour. Thus all land, cattle, machines, houses, furniture, corn, food, and all products of the land, are included in the economical term wealth, because these are all either practically limited in quantity or are the result of human

11

labour; air, on the other hand, could not be described as wealth, because, useful and necessary as it is, it is practically unlimited, and is not the product of human labour.

How do you define LABOUR, economically?

Labour, economically, means productive labour, or labour employed in producing useful objects, i.e., wealth, as above defined.

What is the distinction between wealth and CAPITAL? Is all wealth, capital or is all capital wealth?

Capital means wealth which is employed by its owners, not merely for purposes of production, as, for instance, a hand tool may be by its owner, but which is used, by those possessing it, for the purpose of profit by the labour of others, or as a natural monopoly to tax the consumers.

Then Robinson Crusoe's wheelbarrow or canoe could not be regarded as capital, as is alleged by some economists?

Certainly not, unless Robinson used the wheelbarrow as a means of making profit out of the labour of Man Friday, that is to say, employed the latter to dig out gold or to grow grain and afterward wheel it down to the coast, there to be taken to the markets of the world to be sold for the profit of Robinson himself.

Does, then, the use of the means of production for the employment of the labour of another person constitute those means of production capital?

Strictly speaking, yes, although the mere direct employment of one man by another, as in the case of Robinson and his Man Friday, is of itself but a very rudimentary form of capitalism. The terms CAPITAL, CAPITALIST, and CAPITALISM, as generally used, imply considerable concentrations of the means of production in the hands of one person or a comparatively small number of persons, and the payment of wages for the labour employed in the use of these means of production, in such wise that the total product remains the property of the possessors of the capital used. Thus capital and capitalism imply the existence of a whole series of social conditions in which the users of the tools, the means of production, have no ownership or control over the tools which they use. The terms of the bargain between capitalists and non-capitalists are, therefore, the following: We are the proprietors of the whole produce of our property, our tools, and we agree to pay a small proportion out of this product to you, the actual producers.

What is the meaning of the term VALUE, as used by economists?

A variety of meanings have been given to the term value, but the meaning we attach to it is that of the classical economists, Adam Smith, Ricardo, and others, i.e., value represents the relative amount of average social labour embodied in any useful article.

But does not the usefulness, rarity, or other quality of an article constitute its value?

To some extent, yes; as before stated, various meanings are attached to the term, both by certain economists and in common phraseology. For instance, value is often confounded with the useful quality of an article, its rarity, or even its price in the market. But on examination it will be found that these definitions merely refer to the forms in which value manifests itself, and not to that permanent clement which constitutes value at all times and places where exchange takes place — in other words, that which is its essential character.

But do not people when they speak of value mean the useful quality of an article rather than the amount of labour embodied its that article, or its cost of production its labour?

> That is, undoubtedly, the popular idea, but it is a mistaken one. The true economic value of an article is not determined by its usefulness at all, but, except in cases of a monopoly, by the actual amount of socially-necessary labour embodied in it. This applies to all articles the production of which can be carried on to a practically unlimited extent. Even in cases where value might be supposed to be due to scarcity, as with gold and silver and precious stones, it will be seen on examination that the value is really determined by the amount of average labour expended in producing these things. It is only in the case of articles which cannot be reproduced, such as rare pictures, etc., or where there is a complete monopoly, that the element of scarcity enters into value.

You assert that the basis of all value is the amount of labour embodied its an article, but how can you show that this is the case?

> It is quite clear that the production, that is to say, the making or even the finding, of any useful article involves a certain amount of average labour, and it is equally clear that two persons, exchanging two articles, would seek to get value for value. Say, for instance, one man has a pair of boots, which he wishes to exchange with another man for a quarter of wheat; it is quite clear that as articles of use there is no duality in common between the boots and the wheat, and the only way in which the two parties to the exchange can determine if they are getting value for value is by taking into consideration the amount of labour each article has cost to produce. Wheat and boots are alike the product of labour, that is the one quality which they have in common, that is the one quality by which they can be measured the one against the other, and thus it is clear that it is the amount of labour each article contains which gives it value.

14

That sounds very well in theory, but as a matter of fact people do not judge of the value of the things which they buy in that way, and besides they have no means of judging. How can the man with the wheat tell how much the boots cost in labour to produce, or what does the man with the boots know about the labour-cost of the wheat? Both are in the dark, So is it not more than likely that one or the other gives more value than he gets?

> This may be, and as a matter of fact it is very seldom indeed in the actual exchange of commodities that each one exchanges for precisely its value, but what is lost on the one hand is gained on the other, and so over the whole area of exchanges, the gains and losses cancel each other, and the basis of the total sum of value of all the commodities exchanged would finally resolve itself into the amount of labour they have cost to produce.

But admitting that is so, and that it is the amount of labour put into any article which gives it its value, is it not more than likely that two men making precisely the same kind of things will require a longer or shorter time to make the same article; and thus one article of the same kind will contain very much more labour than another?

> That is quite true, but it is clear that it is only the necessary amount of labour which can give value; therefore it is always essential, in speaking of labour as the basis of value, to bear in mind that it is average labour, or socially necessary labour, which is meant.

You have used the term COMMODITIES once or twice; what do you mean by commodities? Is a commodity the same thing as an article of use; that is to say, are all useful articles commodities?

> Commodities are articles of use produced for exchange. The chief object of practically all labour to-day is the production of useful articles, not for use, but for the market; to be put upon the market for exchange. The owners of the means of production are not greatly

concerned with the utility of the articles which they are engaged in producing; a boot manufacturer, far instance, has no special interest in the production of boots, as boots; what he is concerned with is the production of boots as a commodity, as something to sell, in order to make a profit.

Is the profit of the manufacturer, then, made its the course of exchange on the market?

No. If that were so it would be necessary for each manufacturer or dealer on the market to sell above the cost of production, and that, as we have already pointed out, is impossible. The sellers are also buyers, and although some may buy or sell above the cost, while others may buy or sell below the cost, still, as we have already said, these differences necessarily balance each other, and in the total of exchanges there is neither loss nor profit, although generally the whole body of those engaged in exchange participate in it for the purpose of profit, and generally make a profit.

But if the profit is not made in exchange, how is it made? You say the capitalist only enters into production in order to produce commodities to put upon the market for exchange and that he does this for the purpose of profit, and that he usually makes a profit in the process; yet you say that the profit is not made in exchange. If not, where and how is it made, and where is it? "If Peter Piper picked a peck of pepper, where is the peck of pepper Peter Piper picked?"

In the answer to that question lies the kernel of the whole capitalist system of production for profit, with its exploitation and impoverishment of the proletariat. Profit is not made on the market, but in the workshop, in the mine and the factory. Profit is derived from the surplus value which is wrung from the unpaid labour of the workers.

What is this SURPLUS-VALUE, and how is it created?

Surplus-value is the difference between the cost of labour-power to the capitalist and the amount of labour-power he is able to extract from his workpeople.

What do you mean by LABOUR-POWER?

Labour-power is the capacity for labour inherent in the workman, and it is this capacity or quality which the capitalist buys in the labour market as a commodity. We are assuming a modern capitalist society in which there are no slaves, and the workmen are free. Consequently the capitalist does not buy the workman, neither does he buy labour; that is to say, labour actually expended or in operation. What he buys, when he engages a workman for a given time, is the power to labour contained in the body of the labourer.

You, speak of this labour-power as being bought by the capitalist as a commodity; do you then mean to suggest that it is subject to the same laws as govern other commodities?

Precisely. The labourer and the capitalist meet on the market, the one as seller the other as buyer, in the same way as do the buyers and sellers of other commodities.

Does labour-power, then, exchange according to its cost of production in labour as do other commodities?

Certainly. The exchange-value of labour-power is precisely the same as that of any other commodity, determined by the amount of socially necessary human labour expended in its production; in other words, and in the language usually employed by economists, the return to labour — WAGES — is determined by the cost of subsistence of the labourer. For it is by this subsistence that the labour- power is continually reproduced.

But if the value of labour-power bought by the capitalist is determined by its cost of production in labour, and the commodities this labour-power is employed to produce have also their value determined in the same way, i.e., by the amount of labour incorporated in them, how is this surplus-value of which you have spoken created?

> The capitalist buys labour-power at its cost of production in labour, but the amount of labour which the workman expends, that is to say, the capacity for labour, or the labour-power, which the capitalist buys, and which the workman incorporates in the commodities he produces, is a very much greater quantity than is expended in the production of that labour-power, and it is this difference, a difference which the capitalist gets for nothing, which constitutes surplus-value.

But how does the capitalist secure this surplus-value without paying for it? If the workman is free, why cannot he insist on receiving, not the mere exchange-value of his commodity, "labour-power," but the full value of the labour he expends for the capitalist?

> The capitalist obtains this surplus-value owing to his monopoly of the means of production, which enables him to extend the working day, beyond the hours necessary to produce the subsistence of the labourer; by the employment of machinery, by which the labour of the workman is made more effective; and by the organisation of labour, which has the effect of intensifying the expenditure of labour. The labourer cannot, as a rule, command more than the actual exchange-value of his commodity, that is to say, his cost of subsistence, in return for his labour-although his wages, like the prices of all commodities, sometimes rise above this and sometimes fall below — because, although apparently free, he is really not free. He must sell his labour-power in order to live; he has no other commodity to dispose of, and, having no ownership in or control over the means of

production, he cannot employ himself. Consequently, he has to find a purchaser for his commodity and must accept the terms that purchaser will offer — subject only to two conditions, his own cost of subsistence and the fluctuations of the market. This principle, that the return to labour is determined by the cost of subsistence of the labourer, is generally known as the "Iron Law of Wages."

But has not this law been discarded even by some Socialists?

There have been attempts in some quarters to demonstrate that this law does not actually operate with the rigidity at first claimed for it; but, in truth, it stands as firmly to-day as when insisted upon by Lassalle. The variations or modifications in its operation no more destroy its validity as a general economic law, than the fact that no bodies ever proceed in a direct line, owing to disturbances due to friction, disproves the first law of motion, or the law of gravitation.

Does not the machinery to which you just now referred as being used to make the labour of the workmen more effective, itself produce what you describe as surplus-value?

No. This machinery itself is the product of labour, and is, as we have pointed out, used for the purpose of exploiting labour; but of itself it creates no value. The sum total of the value of a commodity represents the sum total of the average labour employed in its production, including that involved in producing the raw material and the amount of the wear and tear of the machinery used up in the commodity, but the surplus-value comes from unpaid labour only.

Then this surplus-value, as you call it, is merely the profit of the capitalist. Why, then, do you use the term surplus-value, instead of simply speaking of it as profit?

Because the profit of the immediate capitalist employer

19

only forms a portion of the total surplus-value. Out of that total the landlord draws his rent for the land upon which the factory is built; the owner of the factory takes a share himself as rent for the factory; as do also the middleman, the dealer, and all those who handle the commodities for the purpose of making a profit. The fees of the lawyer who maybe engaged in drawing up the deeds, etc., the tithes of the clergy, the salaries of public officers, and in short the rewards or payments of all those who are not themselves engaged in the immediate work of production, these, as well as the remuneration of the contractor engaged in the building of the factory or repairing the machinery; the profit of the broker who sells the raw material, and so on, are all derived from the surplus-value wrung from the unpaid labour of the workers.

But, surely, there are some among the functions even of the State of to-day, as, for instance, the administration of public affairs, which must be paid for from some source, and which, benefit the whole community including the workers themselves; how are these to be remunerated if there is to be no profit at all, or no surplus-value and the workers are paid in full?

It is quite true, as regards the State of to-day, that certain functions are useful and necessary, but many of these functions would be abrogated in the industrial organisation under Socialism. The whole of the administrative work of society would then he necessarily very much simplified, and that which was necessary would, of course, have to be borne, directly or indirectly, by the whole of the members of the social body. Practically, all useful functions then would be public functions — not only those of administration — which would be comprised in the useful work of the community, and each would have to bear his share. This, obviously, involves neither profit nor the capitalistic exploitation of labour.

Then are we to understand that Socialists do not accept the theory of the division of profit, as stated by the orthodox political economy, into Wages of Superintendence, Indemnification for Risk, and Reward of Abstinence (Interest on Loan)?

We certainly do not accept this theory, which is a very lame attempt to explain and justify the profit-making system. Although a portion of profit is spoken of as Wages of Superintendence, it is clear that in so far as such wages are strictly a return for the useful work of management, they are not profit at all, and it is only by a misuse of terms that profit can be so described. The term Wages of Superintendence, however, is generally only a fancy phrase applied by the capitalist to a portion of his profits, and bears no relation whatever to wages in any shape, or to any useful service which the capitalist may perform. As to Indemnification for Risk, the capitalist might so describe a portion of his profit, but as a matter of fact this is purely speculative, as there is no relation between his profit and his risk; while the less said about the abstinence for which he claims to be rewarded the better.

Do you mean to say, then, that the capitalist does not perform a useful function in running a risk for the profit he receives?

For the profit he receives, no. In so far as he exercises the function of management and receives remuneration for this, his remuneration is, as we have already pointed out, not profit at all, but wages of superintendence, and the functions of management would be undertaken by the organised society of the future through its appointed representatives. As to any necessary risk, all individuals would be relieved from this under Socialism, as it would be borne by the whole of society.

But admitting all you say with regard to present conditions, and the exploitation of labour; and granting that some such organisation of society for production for use, as you suggest, were realised, is it not a fact that the total amount of wealth is insufficient to provide anything more than a very poor standard of comfort for all, even if it were equally divided? Admitting that the extremes of squalid poverty and luxurious wealth which we see now were done away with, would it not result in a dead level of mean and sordid existence for all, at best equal to that of the modern artisan or petty clerk?

That is by no means the case. Even under present conditions the total wealth produced would, if equitably divided, amount to a value equal to more than £200 per year per family, which represents a much higher standard than that referred to. But to suppose that any mere distributive readjustment is what is meant by Socialism is to entirely misunderstand what Socialism really involves. Socialism means the complete reorganisation of production as well as distribution. With production scientifically and socially organised, the productivity of labour would be quintupled, and the amount of wealth would be increased in proportion.

But how would the social organisation of labour, as you say, increase its productivity so enormously?

To begin with, by the saving of the tremendous waste of labour which goes on to-day. All the labour employed in advertising, canvassing, travelling for orders, all the printing, railway, warehouse and other work connected with this, is so much wasted labour; it is entirely uuproductive, so far as useful wealth is concerned, and would be quite unnecessary if wealth were produced for use. Then there is the waste of labour involved in the use of obsolete methods, and in the employment of men and women to do work which could be more expeditiously performed by machines, simply because more profit is made by employing the men and women, owing to their labour being cheaper than machinery. And further, there is the inevitable waste of wealth under present circumstances due entirely to the system of production for profit, which makes it often more profitable to destroy wealth or to limit its quantity, rather than, to preserve or increase it. All this would be changed, and the vast mass of labour now wasted would be transferred to useful production, were society organised on a Socialist basis.

But might not this greater productivity be to some extent counterbalanced by greater waste in consumption?

On the contrary, with society properly organised there would be, with the unrestricted enjoyment of wealth, very much less waste — in both labour and material — in consumption. That is to say, the consumption or enjoyment of wealth would be more organised, more social, and less individualistic than it is to-day, with the result that while being the reverse of niggardly it would be infinitely less wasteful than now. For instance, with socially organised enjoyment of wealth it would be possible to have much better food, with the best cooking, serving, etc., for all, and that would be more economical than under the individualistic life of to-day. So with other departments; locomotion would be more economical when social than to-day, where the individual has his own horse or his own carriage; washing would be better and more economically done if socially organised; large dining-halls might take the place of the innumerable little dining-rooms of the present; while the fifty little drawing-rooms of the fifty suburban villas, attended by the fifty "slaveys" of the present time, might be replaced by splendid salons, in which people would meet with much more ease, pleasure and comfort than our present social life affords; and all this without in any way trenching upon the reasonable privacy of individual life. Here it must be distinctly understood that we are not dogmatising as to what will be, but simply suggesting what may be

23

done, in at least one way, to economise consumption by a proper organisation.

Talking of the higher standard of living of the future is it not a fact that the standard of life nowadays, in consequence of the greater productivity of labour through the development of machinery, is very much higher, even among the working classes, than it was, say, fifty or a hundred years ago? Has not Sir R. Giffen shown this to be so by figures?

In a sense that is true, but only to a very limited extent. A certain proportion of the working-class, i.e., the skilled workers, have probably attained a higher standard of living than those of fifty or a hundred years ago; but these are only a very small minority, and the difference between them and the great mass of the working class, whose position has not been improved at all, is proportionately greater. Furthermore, the improvement, even so far as this minority is concerned, has to be discounted by the fact that labour is much more intense than formerly, in consequence of machinery, so that more is taken out of a man in a day's work, and in consequence better living is required in order to keep him in a fit state for working; added to which, employment is, generally speaking, much more precarious, and in a bad season he is worse off than ever before. Then, again, the purchasing power of money has decreased to a very great extent, so that the same nominal wages are not really worth as much as formerly. Sir R. Giffen's figures only go to show that the number of those paying income-tax has increased, from which he appears to conclude that the general body of the people must be better off. But the increase in the number of income-tax payers is fully accounted for by the ordinary growth of population; their proportion to the rest of the community is the same as formerly, and thus the mere increase in their numbers is no evidence at all that the general standard of living is higher.

Is not this fact of the increase is the number of income-tax payers often adduced to show that the Socialist theory, that wealth and capital tend to concentrate into fewer mid fewer hands, is fallacious?

Certainly this is often attempted to be done by those who have never taken the trouble to understand what the Socialist theory of the concentration of wealth and capital really means. But as a matter of fact the increase in the number of income-tax payers proves nothing of the kind. The concentration of wealth and capital into the hands of a comparatively few people, and the corresponding augmentation of the mass of misery, is a fact too glaringly obvious to be disputed, and it is easy to see that the number of people paying income-tax might increase considerably without any increase in the total amount of wealth shared among the general body of these, at the same time that the aggregation and concentration of wealth increased enormously and the masses of the people become still more impoverished. The same argument applies to the statements that are sometimes made with regard to the deposits in the Post Office Savings Bank and similar institutions, and the evidence these afford of the increased well-being of the mass of the people. As a matter of fact, most of these deposits are pitifully small and their owners miserably poor; it is only the few who possess considerable sums, or are much above beggary. So far from these deposits proving the well-being of the workers, they are monuments to their patience in misery. They have been laid up against the ever-threatening "rainy-day," and as soon as that rainy-day comes these small hoards are swept away at once.

The Socialist Conception of History.

But, after all, is this concentration of wealth and capital, of which you speak, so very different from what has obtained in the past? Has there not always been the aggregation of wealth in the hands of a few in all stages of human society?

> Certainly there has been a tendency, to such concentration throughout history, if by history be understood the period when civilisation in Egypt and in Asia supervened upon primitive barbaric or tribal society, up to the present time. In its earlier stages this tendency took the form of usury in its crudest phase. Efforts were made in the early Greek democracies to prevent this usury, and to some extent it was mitigated, but its ultimate result was to bring the land, hitherto common property, into the hands of a comparatively few wealthy families.

You speak of primitive barbaric or tribal society, but in what did tribal society differ from civilised society?

> Briefly, it differed in that its underlying principle was that of social solidarity and communism, at least in the then principal means of production, the land. As to the tribal solidarity, the individual was of no importance; nay, he was scarcely recognised apart from the social whole to which he belonged. Personal rights as such were unknown; for rights, as such, within the society, only existed between groups, between one clan and another, and one tribe and another, or between federations of tribes. The communism of this primitive society did not, of course, preclude the personal possession of tools, weapons, or other articles of personal use, although this did not enter into the actual structure of the community. The sporadic appearance of private property in a society based on primitive communism no more constituted that society individualistic than the sporadic appearance of phalansteries and such-like communistic "experiments" in a society based upon individualism constitutes that society Communist or Socialist. In both cases we have to consider the *essential* structure of the social system in

26

question, and not its *accidental* phenomena.

How do you know that earlier human society was constituted as you say? Where are the proofs of this primitive communism?

To fully answer that question would require a treatise; there are treatises on this subject which may be consulted, but as evidence of the constitution of primitive society being as stated we may instance such examples as survived in the village communities of India before the establishment of British institutions; in the Russian mir, in its older form; in the Arab tribal organisation, and the Javan village communities; in fact, all over the world where the old tribal arrangements of human society, have not been entirely displaced by civilisation in one form or another, may be observed traces of the original primitive communism.

What are the treatises on this subject to which you have referred?

The standard work on this question is the late Emile de Laveleye's book on "Primitive Property." Other works which may be referred to on this matter are those of Sir Henry Maine on "Ancient Law," "Village Communities," "Early Law and 'Customs," Lewis H. Morgan's "Ancient Society," also Gomme's "Village Communities," and several of the writings of the late Professor Robertson Smith. We here only refer to the works on this question which are accessible in the English language; but in other languages there are innumerable treatises on the same subject.

Assuming, then, that your view of early social organisation is the correct one, and that originally the whole of society was based upon group communism, when and how did the change from this primitive communism to civilisation take place?

This change took place at different times in different parts of the world, and a variety of causes have played their part therein. Briefly the change from primitive society may be said to have been generally brought about through the institution of slavery as a consequence of the conflicts between the kinship groups, tribes, or gentes into which primitive human society was divided. Between the tribes — each of which was bound together by real or assumed family ties — there naturally existed considerable hostility, and from this state of things resulted continuous conflicts which necessarily produced slavery. This slavery assumed two more or less distinct forms. Where a migratory tribe or people conquered a settled population, it would, after the fighting was over, allow the vanquished to live on a portion of the conquered lands, on the condition of rendering service to their conquerors, whose serfs they thus became. On the other hand, frequent raids by the tribes or clans on each other produced another kind of slaves; the captives taken in battle were no longer slaughtered on the field when their captors discovered that their labour might be made use of to produce wealth for themselves and these captives became chattel slaves, as much the property of their masters as their horses or their oxen. With chattel slavery or serfdom, as the case might be, thus established, the production of wealth soon outstripped consumption, and with this increase of production, and of the power of production, came inequality in the distribution of goods. The chiefs or leaders were permitted more than their proportion of the general wealth, and thus individualistic or class society began to be established, the first representatives of this class society being usually the chief men of the tribe and their immediate relatives. In the meantime, nomadic peoples had settled down into villages, surrounded by arable and pasture land enclosed by a stockade, and dominated, in hilly countries, by a fortress built on the most prominent height, called in German communities the "bury" or "burg." Such villages were the beginnings of the "city," which at first consisted simply of a federation of tribes living within a given area of limited extent, and thus constituting a people.

How do you regard the Middle Ages? Would you describe the system of society of that tine as individualistic or communistic, barbaric or civilised?

The structure of society during the Middle Ages, the basis of which was what is known as the feudal system, cannot properly be described by any of these terms. The society of the Middle Ages partook to a certain extent of the character of both the primitive barbarism and the later civilisation. It retained many of the features of the older system of society, but these were modified by the new conditions. The idea of common property in land still prevailed to a large extent, with the lord of the manor as in a sense trustee for the general body of the local rural community, but also in a degree as lord and owner. In the latter character he claimed service from the villeins for the use of the land which they held, but they on their side could claim his protection as their military chief. The services rendered included military services, and the lord, although asserting or usurping the rights of ownership, was rather the military head of the community, claiming and rendering service as such, than the owner of the soil with rights and privileges but no duties. Under the feudal system we find, therefore, the land still regarded in a sense as the common property of the inhabitants of each feudal manor, subject to certain restrictions and the superior rights of the lord. The common land of a feudal manor was divided into three parts: the pasture, the arable, and the fallow; the pasture was absolutely common to all the inhabitants, and we find the traces of this common pasture land in our "commons" of to-day; the arable land was parcelled out among the various families, and the fallow was that portion of the arable which was allowed to lie idle from one year to another. In addition to these three divisions of land practically held in common there was the forest or woodland — the unreclaimed land, constituting the actual "waste," from which timber was obtained, firewood was gathered, and into which the pigs and other animals were turned to feed.

But this explanation of the conditions in the Middle Ages only refers to the rural districts; what was the state of things in the towns at that time?

Practically speaking, there were no towns in the earlier period of the Middle Ages. Round certain strongholds collected peasants and handicraftsmen, and these aggregations of industrial life formed the markets which were the centres for such trade as then existed. This, however, does not refer to the towns, numerous in Italy, but few in other parts of Europe, which had continued their existence and had preserved their urban constitution from the period of the Roman civilisation. These, of course, retained the framework of their old industrial, as well as municipal organisation in the narrower sense; hence it was that Italy took the lead of the rest of Europe throughout the Middle Ages in the matter of industry and commerce.

Then did the modern town grow up out of these aggregations of peasants and handicraftsmen around the feudal strongholds to which you have referred?

Yes. The mediaeval towns mostly grew up out of these conditions, and these towns rose to an independent position in the thirteenth century, and reached their zenith in the following century as civic politico-industrial organisations.

How and when, then, did the MEDIAEVAL SYSTEM break up?

It is difficult to assign precise dates for the beginning or ending of any great historical period. But, roughly speaking, the mediaeval system began to show signs of decay in the second half of the fifteenth century, and the process went on rapidly for the next hundred years, till, by the middle of the sixteenth century the change had proceeded so far that the mediaeval system may by that time be regarded as closed, notwithstanding that as survivals many of its institutions continued to exist until long after that period.

What were the causes which brought about this break-up of the mediaeval system?

The institutions of modern capitalism lay in germ in the conditions of the mediaeval system, just as, we Socialists say, the institutions of the future Socialism lie in germ in the conditions of modern capitalism, and it was the growth of these capitalist germs which burst asunder the forms of the mediaeval system, already become old and effete. Various actual and immediate causes may be assigned; among these may be mentioned the taking of Constantinople by the Turks, the invention of firearms and of printing; the discovery of America and the Cape route, and the sudden influx of the precious metals into Europe. The effect of these events and discoveries was to bring about enormous changes in social relations, and to transform the whole conditions of human society.

What form did these changes take?

The first effect of these changes was the opening up of the world market; the aggregation of large accumulations of personal wealth in the hands of individuals; the substitution of money payments for barter, and the rise of the wage system. This aggregation of wealth in the hands of individuals led to the formation of trade or merchant companies or syndicates to exploit the newly opening world market, which were necessarily opposed by the feudal class. As a further consequence of these changes there arose the grouping together of large bodies of wage labourers working for a single employer, and for his profit. This naturally led to the division of labour and the decay of the old trade guilds, whose organisation was a hindrance to this division, and stood in the way of the capitalistic exploitation of labour by this means.

But were these material causes the only ones which operated to bring about the downfall of the mediaeval system and the beginning of commercialism?

There were other causes, certainly, but these we shall have occasion to touch upon later. Those to which we have referred were the chief and primary, although they were reacted upon by other, secondary, causes.

When, then, did the MODERN capitalist system begin?

The modern capitalist system cannot properly be said to have begun before the middle of the sixteenth century. At this period large workshops, in which considerable bodies of workmen were grouped together under one employer for production for profit, began to be organised in the non-chartered towns, or outside the chartered towns themselves, where they were free from the restrictions of the guilds. In the meantime money payments had definitely superseded barter, a change considerably facilitated by the influx of the precious metals from the New World into Europe. By the grouping together of large bodies of workmen under one roof, which was impossible under the guild system, the division of labour was introduced. This paved the way ultimately and by slow degrees to the introduction of the earlier forms of machinery, while the substitution of money payments for barter meant the introduction of a universal equivalent for commodities in all the exchanges in the world market, which was now developing.

In what did the conditions of that time — the middle of the sixteenth century — differ from those of to-day?

The difference is that the forms which then were in their embryonic or primitive stages have now become fully developed At that time, although the labourers were grouped together and their labour began to be sub-divided, this division of labour was as yet in a very primitive stage, and very different from what it is now, and the labour performed was hand-labour assisted by tools or machines worked by hand, instead of the huge, complex, steam-driven machinery of the great industries of to-day. At that time, too, the political power was still almost entirely in the hands of the feudal, or landed aristocracy; the capitalist class had not yet achieved its emancipation from the domination of the older governing class, the bourgeoisie was not then all-powerful, economically, socially, and politically, as it now is.

When and how did this change take place in the conditions of the capitalist system?

Roughly, the beginning of the industrial change may be traced at the commencement of the second half of the eighteenth century, and by the beginning of the nineteenth century it may be said to be fairly established in a number of industries. The political change, which made the capitalist class the dominant political factor, was largely achieved in England in the seventeenth century, with the success of the Cromwellian revolution, carried further by that which placed William of Orange on the throne of England, and fully accomplished with the passing of the Reform Act of 1832. On the Continent of Europe this change may be said to date from the French Revolution.

May we say, then, that the present organisation of society retains the same form in every essential which it assumed at the end of the eighteenth century?

33

By no means. Society has in the century which has intervened passed through enormous changes on all sides; not only industrially and commercially, but politically, intellectually and morally. Industrially, the grouping together of men in factories and workshops has been followed by the grouping together of factories and workshops, and the aggregation of various industries, simultaneously with the concentration of capital in large masses and the development of railways and other huge industrial enterprises. Commercially there has been still greater concentration of capital in the formation of trusts and syndicates, representing not merely trading, as did the syndicates which grew up towards the close of the feudal system, but the grouping, for commercial profit-making purposes, of a large number of great industrial undertakings, generally allied to each other in some way, but frequently entirely dissimilar. This development has culminated in our own day in the formation of the giant octopus-like combinations which promise to bring all the industrial businesses of the world under the control of a mere handful of enormously wealthy capitalists.

The Socialist Conception of Ethics.

So far you have only given the industrial or economic side of the historical development of human society. Do you mean to suggest that the intellectual, religious, artistic, and ethical aspects are entirely subordinate to this?

Certainly not. From the very beginnings of human development the mind of man has had a more or less independent influence on its surroundings. For this reason it is impossible to reduce history to a mere mechanical reflex of its industrial development. To enter at any length into the question of these other phases of human evolution would take us beyond the scope we have set ourselves in this work. It is, however, necessary to say a few words on the subject of ethics, in its connection with Socialism as a system of society.

Is there not a fundamental moral law which is the same in all systems of society?

To a certain extent, yes; but only to so far as all society implies a union of some sort or other, and hence certain broad rules of conduct which are essential to the continuance of this union, but even those broad rules or principles are modified to an almost indefinite extent by changes in the general conditions of social organisation, while many other rules of conduct come into operation and disappear with the varying phases of human society.

Do you mean to say, then, that Socialism has a distinct standard of ethics of its own?

Certainly; and not only Socialism but every other stage of human evolution has its own code of ethics. In early tribal society the ethical object, that is to say the end of conduct, was social; in other words, the highest object of devotion on the part of its members was the group, the tribe or clan, or, in a more advanced stage, the people, or confederacy of tribes. The question of good or evil conduct was determined by whether it served the prosperity, honour or glory of the community, or whether it was inimical to these. As man advanced into civilisation ethical ideas expanded, but at the expense of the narrower social morality of group society. Gradually, as civilisation progressed, the forms of the older group society, becoming obsolete, were superseded by the centralised State organisation, and the ethical centre became shifted from the group to the individual. Good and evil then assumed an absolute value irrespective of society. Religion, which in group society simply meant the conjuration of the spirits of ancestors and of the

35

personified powers of nature in the interests of the tribe, now assumed quite another character, that of the worship of a spiritual deity, who was at once the source and the object of all moral aspiration, directly revealed to the individual conscience. This deity was the central point of the new morality, in which, consequently, man's duty to his fellow men was a matter of secondary consideration. Thus we have first the tribal ethics, the responsibility to society, and in the second place an entirely contrary conception of ethics, the universal or introspective, in which the direct responsibility, was to a divinity, who was the supreme power of the universe, and for whom mankind was but a means of realising himself.

Can you give an illustration of what you mean by universal or introspective ethics?

All religions of the world which were not tribal nor, at least primarily, idolatrous — as it is termed — and which were founded and preached by individual prophets or teachers who claimed to have a divine mission. All these religions were in the main based upon the introspective conception above stated. Judaism, Buddhism and even Mohammedanism, in their purer forms, contained this element very prominently, but Christianity is its great historical expression. The declaration of the founder of Christianity, "The Kingdom of God is within you," gives, in a single phrase, the complete basis of this code of ethics. The Kingdom of God was certainly not "within" the worshipper of a "totem", or emblem of tribal unity; it was indeed "within" the tribe, but outside of any individual member of the tribe.

Then do you suggest that these religions, which superseded the tribal religions, were based upon an individualist ethic?

Most decidedly; inasmuch as the stress of their theory rests in a supposed direct relation of the individual soul with its God, or the soul of the universe, in contradistinction to a direct relation with the social body.

But surely these religions, notably Christianity, embrace moral precepts which are essentially social in their character?

That is perfectly true; but in the case of these religions, these social maxims, in so far as they are not merely survivals, are entirely secondary and derivative; you are called upon to love your brother, whom you can see, by way of practice, and as a preparatory exercise to loving God, whom you cannot see, and so forth.

But is not the word "individualism" used in connection, with ethics generally understood to mean something very different from even the Christian view of social obligations; is it not usually intended to convey the idea of the most narrow material selfishness, as expressed in the phrase, "The devil take the hindmost"?

Yes; with the development of civilisation and the more perfect forms of economic individualism, i.e., capitalism, the older theological ethic — which, though primarily individualistic (from an other-worldly point of view), had yet, as you have remarked, a social side — was superseded in actual practice and in the current theory of life, and became a mere pious opinion, having no practical application.

When did this development of the purely individualistic ethics take place?

This conception of ethics only became the dominant theory within the nineteenth century, with the advent of what has been described as the Manchester school of Political economy. The basis of the theory of that school was the individual scramble for wealth, the cash nexus in place of personal relations, and the dethronement of old-world sentiment in all the departments of life. It was this exaltation of purely material relations between men which led to the phrase, "The devil take the hindmost." Some social reformers regard this ultra-individualistic ethic as the antithesis of the Christian ethic, that is to say, they oppose the Christian ethic to this fully developed individualism. But the real antithesis is not the Christian ethic, which is also in its way individualistic, but the ethic of tribal society on the one side and the ethic of the Socialist society of the future on the other.

What, then, is the ethical conception proper to the Socialist society of the future? Is it not Christian brotherly love?

No. Paradox as it may appear, the Socialist conception of ethics is not this brotherly love, in the Christian sense, although it may, superficially, seem to bear some resemblance to it. On the other hand, nothing is more erroneous than to suppose that Socialism ignores all ethical considerations which are not immediately concerned with the present class struggle in its narrower sense. Our corrupt capitalist society tends more and more to base its ethical judgment — save the mark! — on the mere interest or expediency of the possessing classes, either as a whole or in their more important sections. This is its ethical standard. It is one of the chief duties of the Socialist Party to hold aloft the banner of those fundamental ethical principles which, as we before remarked, are common to all the various forms through which human society has passed. In fact, the maintenance of a truly high ethical standard in public life is one of the most important functions of the Socialist Party of to-day; more important, indeed, than the attainment of any immediate success either generally as a party, or in such matters as might be considered to lie more especially within its sphere.

Can you give an illustration of what you mean by this?

Yes. Two instances in point, from recent and current events, suggest themselves. During the agitation on behalf of Captain Dreyfus it was quite a common thing to hear the remark, "Oh, this is simply a bourgeois affair. Even if the man has been unjustly condemned it is no business of the Socialist Party, which is only concerned when the rights of a workman are assailed." The Socialists of France, with practical unanimity, thought otherwise. They felt by instinct that it was their duty to throw themselves into the breach on behalf of the common principles of justice, and by their vigorous action succeeded in vindicating these principles. Again, the Boer war affords us another instance in which working-class interests were not obviously or directly affected, but where it was a question of asserting the principles of justice on behalf of a small nation of comparatively well-to-do yeoman farmers. Nevertheless, the English Socialist Party with practical unanimity vigorously protested and agitated against the aggressive action of Great Britain, and in favour of the independence of the Republics. Here, again, although, of course, there were very vital issues in the class struggle between Capitalism and Socialism, Bourgeoisie and Proletariat, involved, yet they did not lie on the surface, and it might have seemed politic to have ignored the war as far as possible, with a view of conciliating those among the working classes who had been imposed upon as to the side on which their interests lay by the virulent garbage of the jingo press. The Social-Democratic Party of Great Britain has reason to be proud of its uncompromising attitude on this occasion in defence of international morality against crime.

Are we to understand, then, that the Socialist ethics of the future are no more those of Christianity than they are those of the Manchester school?

Certainly, apart from the fact that the so-called altruistic ethics of Christianity are subordinate to the theological relation of the soul to its God. Even in their very altruism these ethics are one-sided, seeing that they postulate, not as an exceptional incident, but as their root principle, the negation of the self of the natural man, not only to his God, but also to his fellow man. This one-sided, abstract view of the ethical relation has no part nor lot in the very concrete and tangible morality of the Socialism of the future.

But are not the ethics of Socialism essentially altruistic? If that is so, can you have any finer expression of them than is to be found in Christianity, e.g., in the Sermon on the Mount?

Socialist ethics are neither altruistic nor egotistic; they are intrinsically neither selfish nor unselfish. As with other abstractions characterising the phase of human development generally called civilisation — such as the differentiation into separate and even antagonistic classes of the various social functions, of which the cardinal instance is in the two functions of labour and direction separated and embodied in the two antagonistic classes of master and servant — so in ethics we find a purely factitious antagonism set up between the individual and society. This antagonism is based to a large extent on the economic individualism which separates and antagonises the material interests of the individual with his neighbour and with society at large. Given this antagonism, it naturally becomes a virtue on the part of the individual to sacrifice himself habitually for the benefit of others. Where, however, the condition is changed — and in proportion to the degree of this change — the reason for such sacrifice disappears, and to that extent it ceases to be a virtue. The virtue lies in the service rendered to one's neighbour or to society, not in the amount of injury to one's self: thus it would be meritorious to rescue anyone from a burning building, even at the cost of personal suffering or of life itself, and it is difficult to conceive of any set of circumstances in which the reason for such an act might not obtain — but the good would be in the rescue, not in the suffering or sacrifice entailed. Loss, injury, or suffering, is essentially an evil in itself, even if self-inflicted and for a good object. Socialism presupposes a condition of things in which the good of all will mean the good of each; and a society so constituted that the individual cannot serve himself without serving society, and cannot injure society without injuring himself. Thus there will no longer be altruism and egoism, selfishness and unselfishness, existing as antagonistic abstractions, but selfishness and unselfishness must necessarily be alike social in the general run of conduct.

Then Socialism does not presuppose a complete change in human nature and the entire elimination of selfishness, as has been so often asserted?

By no manner of means; on the contrary, Socialism only calls for enlightened selfishness. But the fact that this selfishness *is* enlightened, and recognises that it can serve itself only by serving the common interest, will completely change its character, so that it will cease to be the narrow selfishness of to-day, which so often defeats its own ends. Selfishness passing through the refining fire of economic change ceases to be selfishness and becomes Socialism.

But if this is so, and if the interests of each individual will, by the force of the new circumstances, be best served by serving the common interests, why do the dominant classes of to-day oppose Socialism?

Because, in the first place, their whole education and point of view, inherited and acquired, prevent them seeing that they, in common with the rest of society, would be happier under Socialism. Further, with the more

41

enlightened among them the fact that they are in a better position materially than the majority, and the timidity engendered by the knowledge that at any time they may suffer by a change for the worse, makes them fear any change at all, and prefer a known certainty to an uncertainty, on the principle that a bird in the hand is worth two in the bush. The bulk of these classes, however, are absolutely blinded by their class position to the fact itself that they *would* be happier under Socialism.

Admitting this to explain the attitude of the dominant well-to-do classes, how is it, then, that the great body of the lower middle and working classes are not, as yet, in favour of Socialism?

Because up to the present tune the great majority of these classes are not class-conscious, and hence do not see the direction in which their real interests lie, or that these interests are in antagonism to those of the dominant classes; still less do they see that they are opposed to the existence of a society founded on classes altogether.

You speak of these classes not being class-conscious; what do you mean by that term? Surely if what you call the dominant classes have their own point of view, these others should also have their point of view. Yet we often hear a man declare that although he is not a capitalist, not a bourgeois, but one who has to work for his living, yet he cannot agree with Socialists, but is, on the contrary, an official Liberal, or may be a member of the Primrose League, and as much opposed to Socialism as Rothschild, Carnegie, or any other plutocrat. How do you explain this?

The matter is very simple. The individual who gives this apparently crushing answer that he is not a capitalist and wishes he were, but at the same time cannot agree with the Socialists at all, is still under the domination of the point of view of the ruling classes. Hitherto, throughout history, and at the present time, these classes alone are

42

completely conscious of their own CLASS INTERESTS — that is what we mean by class-consciousness. Indirectly in consequence of this, and directly, in consequence of their dominant economic position, they have hitherto been able to impose their point of view upon the other classes which are not yet class-conscious, and to make this point of view pass current, not for what it is — a class standpoint — but as standing for absolute morality, commonsense, truth, justice — in a word, as representing the welfare of the whole community.

Give an instance of how a dominant class can succeed in imposing its own self-interested "moral" views upon the community at large.

To take one among many, it commonly expresses the utmost horror at anything like a forcible revolution; while the very same persons who do this in one breath, will, in the next, complacently discuss the advisability of waging an unprovoked war for the purpose of asserting national supremacy, or for securing fresh commercial outlets. The horror at the human suffering entailed, so eloquently expressed in the first case, evaporates under some phrase such as "necessity" or "inevitability" (which, being interpreted, means desirability from their own class point of view) in the other. They well know that, as possessing classes, they have everything to lose and nothing to gain in a domestic revolution, while in a foreign war they often think they have a great deal to gain, and, as they hope, very little to lose. Once more, on the occasion of the assassination of any potentate or statesman, the public opinion of the possessing class and its organs is lashed up to a white heat of artificial fury and indignation against the perpetrator, while they have nothing but approbation for the functionary — military or civil — who puts to death a fellow-creature in the course of what they are pleased to call his duty; as, for instance, in the execution in cold blood, after the event, of the two Boer prisoners simply for attempting to escape at Pretoria. Evidently force and bloodshed, when contrary to the interests of the possessing class, is a monstrous crime, but when it is in their favour it becomes a duty and a necessity.

How has the dominant class been thus able to impose its own point of view upon the other classes? Has this been done deliberately on their part — so to say, of malice aforethought?

In the past, the overpowering influence of the dominant class has been in the main unconscious, it has been due to the position of that class, and has not been deliberately imposed. Until the development of capitalism, however, and of the consciousness of class interests as such, the leaders of the dominant or possessing class by means of their control over press, pulpit and platform, deliberately seek to impose as truth, morality and religion the ideas which suit their purpose and best serve their class interests.

That being so, are we then to understand that the whole of history so far has been written from the point of view of the dominant class of every age?

Most assuredly so, and this applies to well-nigh the whole of the sources of past history. For example, in the Book of Kings, and the other so-called historical books of the Old Testament, ancient Hebrew history is given us from the point of view of the wealthy influential Jehovistic priesthood of Jerusalem, and of the narrow nationalism which was its ideal side. It is from their standpoint that men are lauded or condemned. Again, the history of Catiline, who represented the disinherited classes of Rome against the tyranny of wealth, and its exclusive dominance in the State, has been handed down to us as the history of a scoundrel, opposing the forces of public order. Coming to medieval history, we have the case of

44

the English peasant rebellion of 1380, the leaders of which have been uniformly maligned by chroniclers and historians, as have also, to speak of a later period, the men of the German peasant insurrection, together with John of Leyden and the Anabaptists of Munster. Turning once more to modern times, we have only to remember the vilification of all the popular leaders of the French Revolution or of the Paris Commune of 1871. So it is throughout history. Whether good or bad, events and characters have been judged, and the verdict of history passed upon them solely from the point of view of the dominant class of the period in which they appeared. The whole of history will have to be re-written in the future from the point of view of the people of an epoch, and no longer from that of its dominant classes.

Seeing the importance of this point and the very widespread notion that no man who is not a capitalist can be expected to hold capitalistic views of social relations, will you in a few words recapitulate your position on this matter?

To begin with, throughout civilisation — that is, that period of human evolution in which class divisions are the special characteristic — the dominant class, necessarily, by reason of being the dominant class, imposes its ideas, principles and views upon the whole of any given society. Such a society must necessarily partake of the character and be moulded by the principles which serve the interests of its master class, or cease to exist as such. This imposition of the will and principles of the dominant class may be done consciously or unconsciously. In the earlier stages of civilisation this class used the speculative and religious beliefs which were held by the general body of the people, and even by itself to a large extent, as a cover and justification for its supremacy as a class; this it did in the main (although not always) unconsciously, and without malice aforethought. Nowadays, however, there is

45

no illusion in the matter; the dominant classes, working on hereditary feelings, deliberately mislead or "bull-doze" the rest of the people, and this is why the man whose class position should make him a Socialist remains as thoroughly reactionary as any member of the dominant class until he becomes class-conscious, i.e., conscious of his class position and the essential antagonism between the interests of his class and those above him in the economic scale. He then sees through the whole fraud of bourgeois religion, morality and politics. Therefore, although the bulk of the recruits to Socialism will come from the working classes, it makes not the slightest difference intrinsically to a man being a Socialist, whether he be rich or poor, so long as he accepts the principle of the class struggle, and recognises the historical function of the proletariat, as a class, to found a new society. A "horny-handed" son of toil is often an enemy of Socialism and of his class, while a wealthy man may be an ardent and sincere Socialist and champion of the workers, devoting his whole life to the task of their emancipation.

The Socialist Conception of the Universe.

But if Socialism has a code of ethics of its own, has it also it religion of its own? What is the Socialist conception of the universe?

Socialism primarily accepts the theory of evolution in its fullest extent. It bases its view of the universe upon positive science and reasoned conclusions. Socialism has hitherto been materialistic, as opposed to antiquated conceptions based on theological dogma — but not with the idea of erecting materialism itself into a dogma. It will probably continue to be so until, and in so far as, modern scientific materialism is generally shown to be, by itself, an inadequate conception of the universe. It is not, however, with our province to go into the details of this subject here.

But does not the doctrine of evolution include what is known as Darwinism, with its theory of the struggle for existence and the survival of the fittest? And is not this opposed to the co-operative conception of Socialism?

The doctrine of evolution certainly does include Darwinism in the fullest sense of the term; but the discoveries and teaching of Darwin are not in opposition to Socialism. The struggle for existence and survival of the fittest assume a variety of forms, besides that of the struggle of individuals with each other. There is the elemental struggle with the forces of nature, the struggle between classes, the struggle between races, and, most important of all, the struggle between different systems of society; in all of which the side best adapted to the circumstances in which the struggle takes place is the one to survive. The mere struggle between individuals is a very crude and elementary form of that struggle for existence which may be regarded as one of the laws of life and movement; and under Socialism this will assume a higher and totally different form. In primitive society the struggle was not between individuals but between groups (tribes or clans); in future society, the society of Socialism, the struggle will be between different methods and forms of organisation for the exploitation of natural resources in the general interest, or for the most effective maintenance of the common social life.

How are you to secure the continued evolution of the human race and the development of its highest qualities if you destroy or diminish the existing supreme incentive of strenuous competition under the present system of free competitive effort?

This question, which is often asked, and as frequently answered, is based upon a complete misconception of

47

existing social conditions. It is a fallacy to suppose that competition alone has at any time brought out the highest qualities of humanity. Even where the struggle for existence has been most keen, the victor in the struggle has almost invariably been aided by co-operation in some form or other. Moreover, all competition, as in the historic case of the Kilkenny cats, inevitably tends to its own extinction. It necessarily results, by the defeat of the various competitors, in some form of monopoly. As a matter of fact, at the present time, all purely natural forms of competition have disappeared, and such competition as exists does not encourage the development of the best, the strongest, the most able, or the most wise. It is an incentive to nothing but swindling, chicanery, and fraud. In the present social system, where the individual gains only at the expense of others, there is no incentive to the artist or the inventor to create or invent anything which will directly contribute to the general social well-being. The inventor, as a rule, meets with little or no reward, or if he does, it is for an invention which, while bringing profit to a few will inflict untold misery upon thousands, as in the case of the great industrial inventions of the last century. In a system of society, however, in which all production is carried on for use, and where every invention will confer a social benefit, there will be the incentive, not only of a possible individual reward, but of the knowledge that the whole of humanity will benefit, and nobody suffer, by the invention. It may also be pointed out that not only does the present system offer no incentive to the development or exercise of genius, but that no great invention, and no great work of art, has ever been achieved as the mere result of incentive in the shape of the hope of a personal reward. This does not, as might be supposed, apply only to the fine arts, where it is true absolutely and without any reservation whatever, it also applies, with almost equal truth, to industrial inventions.

Indeed, so far from any incentive being offered to invention by competition, at the present time, many useful mechanical inventions are kept out of use in the interests of the monopolies which have grown, up through competition. So that whatever may be said for present conditions the incentive to the continued evolution of the human race and the development of its highest qualities could not possibly be less under Socialism than it is to-day. For the simple reason that nothing could be less calculated to the development of the highest qualities in humanity than the existing system of society.

Socialist Internationalism.

You referred just now to the struggle between races as being one of the typical forms in which the struggle for existence, resulting in the survival of the fittest, has manifested itself. Surely this struggle between races is a matter of vital importance to-day, with the intense commercial rivalries between modern civilised nations. How are these international struggles to be eliminated? What is the Socialist view as to future international relations?

Socialism is essentially international. It recognises no distinction between the various nations comprising the modern civilised world. "My country, right or wrong," the expression of modern patriotism, is the very antithesis of Socialism. It is the most sacred duty of the Socialist to prevent his country from going wrong. But if he cannot prevent it, if it allows itself to be seduced into dealing unjustly with other countries, then the Socialist naturally wishes for the defeat and punishment of his country. For it is necessary to remember that Socialism is utterly opposed to imperialism, which would reduce as many nations, as possible under the flag of one nation and the domination of a particular race. Even where such agglomerations of nations under the flag of the strongest

49

take place pacifically, it is equally opposed to the internationalism of Socialism or Social- Democracy. This internationalism means liberty and equality between nations as between individuals, and amalgamation as soon as feasible and as close as possible under the Red Flag of Social-Democracy, which does not recognise national distinctions or the division of progressive humanity into nations and races. The universal international organisation, as manifested in its representative, or governing body, may reasonably, take its rise from an international court of arbitration, originally established to settle disputes between nations, and gradually tending to absorb new functions previously exercised by the various national legislatures.

But what is the attitude of Socialism towards backward races, savage and barbaric peoples who are to-day outside the civilised world?

The position of Socialism towards these races is one of absolute non-interference. We hold that they should be left entirely alone to develop themselves in the natural order of things; which they must inevitably do or die out. This is the attitude of Socialism towards these races, not only from considerations of justice, or on abstract ethical grounds, but also for Socialist economic reasons, as the expansion of capitalism beyond its present limits means the buttressing of the present system of society and the extension of its lease of life. For this reason all the Socialist parties of the world have by instinct thrown the whole force of their opposition against colonial expansion in any form or shape. Socialists are in this respect eminently "Little Englanders," "Little Francers," and "Little Germaners."

But is it not natural that civilised nations should protect those of their members who go among the savage and barbaric races as missionaries, traders, explorers, and others whose ostensible

50

object it is to spread Christian civilisation, among them?

Yes, it is perfectly natural, from the point of view of the dominant classes, who to-day control the destinies of the civilised world; and it is also natural for the barbaric races to resent having the religion, the shoddy wares, and other disagreeable products of civilisation forced upon them, and to give practical form to this resentment. It is rather the duty of Socialists to support the barbaric races in their resistance to aggression, than to acquiesce in the fraudulent pretences by which the people referred to insinuate themselves into favour among those whom it is their object to betray.

What do you mean by fraudulent pretences in the case, say, of missionaries?

The object of the explorer is to spy out the land; to find means of entry for the future operations of the trader and the exploiter. The missionary is the John the Baptist of the capitalist, who goes to prepare the way before him. The trader follows the explorer and the missionary, to secure for the capitalist class as much of the produce of the country as he can grab, and to establish as large a market as circumstances will permit. Last of all comes the general and establishes a "protectorate" over the country by means of "military operations."

But surely many missionaries are sincere in their belief that they are conferring a benefit upon these unenlightened peoples, by devoting themselves to preaching the Gospel among them?

Generations ago, this may have been to a large extent the case; and even now occasional instances will be found to which this remark would apply. But now-a-days missionaries are, generally speaking, the conscious or, at best, the semi-conscious tools of their masters — the churchwardens, deacons, and religious world generally, who wish to find secure markets for the products of their

51

factories, and profitable outlets for their surplus capital, the industrial exploitation of the land, in the shape of mines, railway concessions, etc. We have seen in the past how the missionaries have been the lever by which a quarrel with China was concocted; and this convenient habit of picking quarrels is by no means the least of the services the missionaries render to the capitalists.

Socialism and Politics.

This being your attitude with regard to international relations, what is the Socialist position in connection with internal or domestic politics?

> Generally speaking the position of the Socialist Party in every civilised country is one of hostility to the existing political order. That order is based upon private property in the means of production, and its function is to maintain and defend that property in the interests of the dominant class. Hence the existing political order is in antagonism to Socialism.

From the foregoing, then, we are to understand that Socialism cannot afford to ignore existing political forms, as is sometimes asserted by Fabians on the one side and Sentimentalists on the other?

> Certainly. Socialists are essentially thorough-going Republicans. Socialism, which aims at political and economic equality, is radically inconsistent with any other political form whatever than that of Republicanism. By this we do not mean any existing republican constitution, which is a quite superficial matter, but that the principle of republicanism is essential to Socialism. Monarchy and Socialism, or Empire and Socialism, are incompatible and inconceivable. Socialism involves political and economic equality; while Monarchy or Empire essentially imply domination and inequality.

You say that your attitude is one of hostility to the existing political order, and that Socialism is essentially Republican. How, then, do you propose to give practical effect to this hostility and to demonstrate your Republicanism in a tangible form? Do you purpose organising, and waiting for, a revolutionary outbreak?

Socialism is essentially revolutionary, politically and economically, as it aims at the complete overthrow of existing economic and political conditions. We should organise and be prepared for what might be described as a revolutionary outbreak, certainly; but we do not need to wait for it. As we have endeavoured to show, the economic changes which are taking place, and the corresponding changes in other conditions, are bringing about a revolutionary transformation in human society, and what we have to do is to help on this development and to prepare the way for it.

How do you reconcile your revolutionary principles with your practice of tinkering with existing conditions as shown by your participation in current political action and the palliative programmes put forward by the Socialist parties of the various countries?

While organising and working for the complete overthrow of the capitalist system, Socialists everywhere recognise it to be their duty, as far as possible, to mitigate the evil effects of existing conditions, not only for the good directly effected by such mitigation, but also because, by the restriction of the exploitation and impoverishment of the proletariat, they must necessarily help on the economic and social development for which they are working. Thus it is incumbent upon us to enter into the active political life of the day in order to press forward such measures as better and free education, and free maintenance for the children; the raising of the age at which children should enter the factory; the strict limitation of the working day; a minimum wage, and,

53

where necessary, maximum price; prohibition of poisonous occupations, and the general protection of the lives and limbs of the working classes in their work; the public construction of healthy workmen's dwellings, etc. Socialists advocate and support such measures as these as being calculated not only to palliate the worst evils of capitalism, but also to raise the physical, moral and mental status of the working-class, and to better fit them for the struggle for their emancipation — at the same time that such measures would in many cases help on that emancipation by restricting the limits of private, and increasing the area of public, property.

But in the historical development of the Socialist movement has not this participation in what is sometimes called practical politics proved to be a considerable danger?

Very much so, indeed, but it is a danger the movement is bound to run, unless it would sink into mere Utopianism. A revolutionary movement must risk something, but it should profit by experience, and the dangers arising from participation — with a strict adherence to fundamental principles — in the active political life of the day are not nearly so great as those resulting from an avoidance of political action. That amounts to sheer "impossibilism." It is indeed the theory of the Anarchists. But it is almost invariably found that those who start out as Anarchists with the idea of cutting themselves adrift from the contamination of all political activity, in the practical sense, as being mere mild tinkering with the present system, strange as it may seem, land themselves ultimately in some weak reform movement of an infinitely milder character than the proposals of the most opportunist Social-Democrat against whom they have formerly inveighed.

Then we are to gather from the above that Socialism presupposes political and economic democracy? Does this democracy imply absolute equality between the sexes?

Economically, certainly; for equal service equal remuneration or credit, material or moral, to man or woman; and it is perfectly certain that the establishment of such economic equality must necessarily produce very material and radical changes in the position of woman and the relations between the sexes. The precise nature of these changes it would be rash at the present time to predict. The subject, however, in this connection, is beset with fallacies, especially false analogies. People forget that the relation of sex is largely unique in its character as implying an organic difference, and not a mere social one, and hence quite distinct from the relation of class or of race. The relation of man to woman has none but the most superficial analogy to that of an exploiting class with an exploited class, or of a dominant race with a subject race. And yet this thinnest of superficial analogies, hardly worthy the name of analogy at all, is constantly being reasoned from with axiomatic dogmatism, which would be not even justified were the analogy complete at all points.

But leaving aside the question of future conditions between risen and women; what is the position of Socialism towards the question of marriage as at present constituted?

The existing marriage relation is determined as such relations have always been determined, throughout human development, by the general economic institutions of the existing society. The existing monogamic relation is simply the outcome of the institution of private or individual property. It has developed, in proportion to the accentuation of the institution of private as against communal property. When private property ceases to be the fulcrum around which the relations between the sexes turn, any attempt at coercion, moral or material, in these relations (such as is implied in laws mechanically and compulsorily prescribing their conditions, as do the marriage laws of to-day), since it would have no reason for its existence, must necessarily become repugnant to the moral sense of the community.

Socialism and the Labour Movement.

Apart from this question of sex, are we to understated that Socialism champions and allies itself with every movement for class and race equality, and for the improvement of the present condition of the working classes?

> That depends entirely upon the character of such movements. All which tend in the direction of Socialism are encouraged and assisted by Socialists. All which, no matter how reasonable or attractive they appear on the surface, are essentially antagonistic to Socialism, Socialists are bound to oppose as misleading and dangerous.

Can you give some illustrations of these various movements?

> To begin with, Trade Unions call for the support of Socialists, in so far as they are manifestations of the class struggle, and represent an organised effort of the working class to prevent or restrict their exploitation by the capitalist class. The Co-operative movement, again, to the extent to which it aims at organising industry independently of the capitalist class, has the sympathy and support of Socialists. On the other hand, so-called Thrift and Temperance movements, and Malthusianism, in so far as they aim at reducing the standard of living for the workman, training him to work for a lower wage, and so cheapen labour and increase the margin of profit of the capitalist class, are essentially antagonistic to Socialism. Once the choice is given between sensual pleasures and sports and intellectual and artistic enjoyments, the regeneration of the working class will evolve without

exciting coercion.

Surely Trade Unionism, as the one organised expression of the working class in opposition to the capitalist class, is the essential embodiment of working-class ideas, and should everywhere not only command the support of the Socialists as representing the class movement, but should be recognised as paramount in that movement?

> The English Trade Union organisation is in a sense a survival of an earlier stage than the present in the class struggle. The tendency is for that struggle to become more and more political, and in so far as trade unions ally themselves with the political working-class movement, they retain their place as active factors in the conflict. In so far, however, as they allow themselves to be dominated by old ideas and abstain from any participation in political life, they become useless and even reactionary.

Is there, then, an antagonism between Socialism and Trade Unionism when the latter becomes, as you say, useless and reactionary?

> There is no antagonism between Socialism and Trade Unionism except when the trade union becomes politically retrograde, Even in that case it is a question in the main of policy and methods, which will be altered as Socialist influence makes its way in the union. The trade unions generally must sooner or later become — they already in some instances are to-day — part and parcel of the working-class Socialist movement, or must cease to exist, as class organisations.

But surely the Co-operative movement is essentially Socialist?

> Co-operation is in its inception Socialist. That is to say, that all co-operation implies co-operative effort and social union. But the general practice of co-operation to-day is of a joint-stock enterprise, on the part of a number of

petty shareholders. Modern industrial co-operation is, therefore, little more than playing at capitalism. Under existing conditions no business enterprise can succeed except on competitive lines, and so the co-operative societies of to-day simply represent co-operation to compete, with capitalist concerns, on capitalist conditions. They must successfully compete or go under. Thus, while conferring some slight advantage on their members, co-operative societies have little connection with the present working-class movement, except where they are subsidiary to that movement and serve to help supply it with funds; as in the case of the co-operative societies of Belgium.

You referred to the "So-called Thrift and Temperance movements" and "Malthusianism" as being antagonistic to Socialism. Are they not generally regarded as agencies for the improvement of the moral and material conditions of the working classes?

It is quite true that these schemes are generally so regarded, but as a matter of fact they afford excellent examples of what may be described as bogus working-class movements. Under present circumstances the more frugal, thrifty, and abstemious, working people, as a class, become, the more cheaply they have to live, the more cheaply they have to sell their labour power to the capitalist class. Wages being determined by cost of subsistence, the lower the standard of life of the workman the lower are his wages. This applies to all the various nostrums (including Malthusianism) which aim at reducing the cost of living to the workman.

State and Municipal Enterprise.

But is not this attitude towards these reform movements somewhat in contradiction to the Socialist approval of State and

58

Municipal enterprise such as involves cheap transit, improved and cheaper dwellings, free education and free maintenance for the children, etc., all of which imply reduced cost of living to the workman?

It is quite true that to some extent such measures as you have mentioned would have the effect of reducing the cost of living to the workman, and so far they are on all fours with the "reform" movements which we have condemned as antagonistic to Socialism. Nevertheless, they are supported by Socialists because they would materially improve the conditions of the working class, and are, besides, stepping-stones towards Socialism, and restrictions and limitations of capitalist exploitation and domination.

Does this apply to all State and Municipal enterprises which may be undertaken under the name of "Social Reform"?

Certainly not. There are many so-called "Social Reforms," State and Municipal, which are not distinctly of advantage to working-class interests, and may even be inimical thereto. There are, for instance, proposals for taxation reform, which would mean mere burden — shifting — lifting the burden of taxation from the shoulders of one section of the dominant class and placing it upon another, but affording no benefit to the worker. Thus, what is called the taxation of land values would afford relief to those capitalists who derive their profits directly from industrialism, at the expense of those who draw their incomes from land, but would not in any way reduce the amount of surplus-value taken from the working class.

But do not the working class pay the rates and taxes?

No. Rates and taxes are paid out of the surplus-value taken from the workers by their exploiters. As already explained, the return to the workers — their wages — is determined by their cost of subsistence, regulated by competition in the labour market; consequently they have nothing wherewith to pay taxes, and whether these be high or low, or whoever has to pay them directly, the position of the worker remains the same. He gets, on the average, his subsistence, that is all.

Does this hold good with regard to municipal enterprises, such as municipal gas, water, tramways, electric lighting, etc., the profits of which are used to reduce the rates? Is not such a reduction of rates of special benefit to the working class and to the community generally?

> No. Generally speaking, the reduction of rates is of no benefit whatever to the working class. Rates are levied upon property, and to devote the proceeds of municipal undertakings to the reduction of rates is simply to use them, as we have already stated, as means for making profit for the propertied class.

What, then, is the position of Socialism generally towards the extension of municipalism and municipal enterprise?

> Socialism is distinctly in favour of the extension of the municipalisation of those services which are municipal, as of the nationalisation of others. But this municipalisation or nationalisation must proceed on right lines, and for a practical object.

What, then, should be the object of municipalisation and nationalisation?

> The primary object should be the most economical provision of the best possible public services. The general well-being should be the first consideration to be served, having due regard to the welfare of each and all engaged in these services. The idea of profit either in the shape of interest on loans, or of reduced rates and taxes, should be eliminated altogether. National and municipal enterprise

is to be encouraged in every way in which the foregoing principle is kept in view, in which it involves the extension of public property, and in which it serves in a practical form the improvement of the condition of the working class.

Conculsion.

Socialists constantly assert their belief in the speedy downfall of the present system, and the near advent of Socialism; what are their reasons for this belief?

There are many grounds, small and great, upon which we base: our conclusions in this respect, The chief economical ground is that all the facts go to show that capitalism has reached the furthest term of its development. If it continues to exist it can only be by a sort of artificial prolongation of its life through a suspension of that social development which in the normal course should effect its transformation into collectivism, as it is difficult to see any further organic changes through which it can pass. We might point out as one of the signs of the end of capitalism, that it is already being controlled more and more completely by its financial side. In its earlier and immature stages, it is the commercial aspect which is dominant; it is the merchant who travels from city to city to buy and sell and get gain (mainly with raw materials), that is its typical representative. Little progress beyond this stage was made either in Antiquity or throughout the Middle Ages. During the subsequent development, the employer of labour, the manufacturer, became the "predominant partner" until, in the heyday of its vigour, throughout the great industry of the nineteenth century, the manufacturer, or in other words, the industrial side of capitalism, controlled the whole system. Now, at the opening of the twentieth century, we see the supremacy of the old industrial capitalist in its turn threatened, and even more than threatened, by the mere man of money-the financier — of which the Rockefellers, the Rhodeses, and the Pierpont Morgans are types. This domination of the FINANCIAL side, of capitalism over the COMMERCIAL and INDUSTRIAL respectively, which means the reign of trusts and big combines, denotes the last stage of capitalism, and the final extinction of the last useful function of the capitalist as the direct organiser and immediate supervisor of industrial processes. (The organisation of the financial capitalist is of, quite a different order.) The trust system obviously spells the reduction of the wealth of the world under the control of a few gigantic cosmopolitan capitalists and syndicates; and from this to the removal of these possessing money-lords, and the assumption of the productive wealth of the world by democratic society organised to this end, is only a step.

But the foregoing, true as it may be, only refers to the material development, and you have said that Socialism is something more than an economic theory. Are we to understand, nevertheless, that Socialism is merely sordid and material, and has no regard for the more ideal side of human interests?

By no manner of means. The Socialist recognises, far more than others, the higher ideals of human life as being its true end. But the Socialist, if he be worthy the name, refuses to be befooled himself or to befool others, with vapid phrases about the scorning of the material side of life, plain living and high thinking, and so on. He knows that to place mankind in a position to realise its higher aspirations, it is necessary to ignore these "spiritual" things in their present, largely bogus, form, and to direct his attention primarily to the securing of the material ends of life by material means — a proceeding so much despised in theory by those who have already attained these material ends in practice. In the words of St. Paul, "That which thou sowest is not quickened except it die," and much of what now passes for the "higher interests" will undoubtedly, to follow out the metaphor, have to die and be buried, in the rich soil of new material conditions, before it can be quickened into real life, and blossom forth in the more perfect ideals of the future. Material conditions form the fundamental basis of human existence. When these become common property, free to all, and abundant for all, they will cease to have that importance they now possess; the sordid struggle for mere material things will disappear; free play will be given to man's higher faculties, and the struggle, competition, or emulation between man and man will be for the realisation of his highest conceivable aspirations. With his mind freed from the dreary cares now imposed by the perpetual struggle for daily bread, man will bend his thoughts on nobler things. Absolute master of the material circumstances of life, his Will must dominate, and be no longer dominated by them, and such opportunities of existence, such scope for mental and moral gratification, such ideals and aspirations will open up before him as are at present, inconceivable.

Does Socialism, then, represent a final phase of human development, beyond which nothing further is possible?

All we claim for Socialism is that it is the next summit which has to be attained in man's progress onward and upward. This summit hides from our view all that may lie beyond; we only know that a return to Individualism as we see it to-day and as it has been to a greater or less extent throughout history, will be impossible. The goal of Socialism once having been attained, the ground gained will never more be lost. What further developments in human social organisation, beyond those Socialist forms which we can conceive of at the present time, may be in

63

store, we not know. It is enough for us to work for our ideal — the Socialism we can foresee; in which we know must be realised the nearest approach, since man first appeared on this planet, to the state pictured by the Syrian dreamer, on the Aegean sea, in the first century of the Christian era, when he wrote of a time when the tears shall be wiped from all eyes, when there shall be no more grief — "neither sorrow nor crying, neither shall there be any more pain."

Appendix: Class-Consciousness and Class-War

The terms at the head of this article are so often used in our propaganda and are so exceptionally misunderstood, willingly or otherwise, that it may be worth while to briefly consider what we mean by them.

To some persons the phrase class-consciousness means something very philosophic and mysterious, and the word class-war something very brutal and reprehensible. As a matter of fact, the two phrases are simply general expressions for every-day facts of civilisation. Take class-consciousness: every class in a class-society may be class-conscious, i.e., it may as a class, through an overwhelming majority of its members, possess a strong sense of its common class-interests down to their remoter ramifications. Even sections of a class (e.g., particular trades) may be class-conscious, though here the solidarity is not sufficiently far-reaching to stand alone and usually merges in its wider issues in the consciousness of the class itself. But if there may be a sectional consciousness within one class there may also be a sense of solidarity between allied classes,, in which case there is a common feeling of class interest engendered, or in other words a common class-consciousness between these two allied classes. Thus, to-day, we see the remains of the old feudal class, the landed aristocracy, on main issues completely at one with the middle classes, even the small middle class having capitulated without conditions to this combination. We have therefore, to-day a reactionary force of a power hitherto unparalleled in the history of class-society.

But it must be remembered that every class seeks to impose its own class point of view, when it can, upon the whole community. This it succeeds in doing in proportion to the want of class-consciousness in the classes below it. The average British workman swallows complacently the moral judgments of the capitalist press when it teaches him that the robbery of the Transvaal from the Boers and the murder of prisoners by the British forces are righteous acts, while the anarchistic slaying of a potentate or statesman is a blood-curdling-enormity, to adequately describe which words fail. It is possible to work this arrangement now, because the small middle-class has merged its class-consciousness in that of the possessing classes as a whole, while the bulk of the working classes (of this country at least) have not yet attained to a class consciousness at all. But it was not always so.

To keep to the particular line of illustration above given, in the forty-eight period, and even later, the Mazzinis and Orsinis, who preached and, in the latter case, practised, the doctrine of the righteousness of the assassination of rulers, were the idols of the small middle-class democrat. In Zürich there is a much-frequented Cafe Orsini, which was established at that time. Fancy today a Cafe Czolgoz or a Hotel Bresci! The same remark applies along the whole line of ethical judgement. The idea of crushing the independence of weaker nation would have revolted the whole of the lower middle class; to-day it cheerfully accepts the situation, and is even enthusiastic over the interests of the big capitalists. In short, the "reactionary mass" over against working-class interests – which Marx prophesied would come, and which has in these latter days been realised – has things, pretty much all its own way. Those who oppose it are mainly confined to the Socialist Party. And it is precisely the Socialist Party which represents the class-consciousness of the modern working-class. It is the centre whence this class-consciousness is destined to radiate till it has absorbed the whole class.

Now, speaking from an ethical point of view, class-consciousness may be either good or bad. And whether it be good or bad does not necessarily depend on the class. What, then, it may be asked, does it depend on? I answer, on the fact whether the class, rightly or wrongly, identifies its own interest *in sincerity* with that of the whole of society. Time was, at the end of the eighteenth and during the earlier decades of the nineteenth century, when the middle classes (certainly the lower middle classes) answered to this test. At that time economic development hid from their eyes the crucialness of the distinction between the middle and working classes. The men of the Mountain in the French Revolution, the early English Radicals, the bulk of the advanced party in all countries in 1848 (for the class-consciousness of the proletariat was then only just beginning) – nay, most even of the Chartist leaders themselves – in perfect sincerity conceived the working classes and the whole of humanity as embraced within the purview of the class-consciousness of at least, the poorer sections of the middle classes. Men like Mazzini, who in view of his scandalous action with regard to the Commune one is sometimes tempted to regard as a humbug, probably in all sincerity took this view.

The differentiation between the two classes was not at that time sufficiently obvious to force itself upon the notice of any observer who was not, like Marx and Engels, especially on the look-out for it. Now that it has become evident, the class-consciousness of the *bourgeoisie* means nothing more practically than a sense of selfish class-advantage and the effort to obtain it. This is what we really mean when we say that the idealism has gone out of the middle classes, which is the same as saying that the aspirations of the middle class, as such, have ceased to be ethical. This does not exclude the existence of individual Liberals and Radicals who are blind and belated, and hence sincerely hold the old view still.

In the same way there was, doubtless, a time when the thinking men among the feudal aristocracy of the Middle Ages sincerely believed, in accordance with their theological outlook on the world generally, that the feudal hierarchy was a divinely-appointed order of things, the ideal perfection of which represented the highest conceivable good of the human race as a whole. St. Louis may have been of this type. By the 16th century, and earlier, however, the feudal classes had become conscious seekers after their own class-interests against the rest of the world.

Now, the class-consciousness of the proletarian of to-day in so far as he "raises the principle of his class to be the principle of his age" (to use the words of Lassalle) is an ethical class-consciousness. This is the case necessarily with Social-Democrats, who have no ill-will towards individuals of other classes – save perhaps where they are the avowed champions of or when they exacerbate the evils of the present system – but who aim at a revolution which means the abolition of class-society, a revolution which will do away with the condition of proletarianism altogether and inaugurate a truly human society.

On the other hand there is a form of proletarian class-consciousness which is undoubtedly unethical, and which expresses itself in throwing bombs in theatres, cafes, &c., merely because the bulk of their frequenters happen to be non-proletarians. This class-consciousness arises in mere class vindictiveness and nothing beyond. (We may here remark that the slaying of persons actively representing the existing order of society, however much we may disapprove it, comes under quite a different category to this.)

Class-consciousness, implicit or explicit, necessarily gives rise to one or another form of the class war. The class war as waged by the Social-Democrat, while it has as its immediate objective a class-purpose, viz., the advancement of the working class in its political and economic struggle with the privileged and possessing classes of to-day, has as its ultimate goal the realisation of the highest interests of mankind as a whole.